W9-BFL-105

DATE DUE

GALLINAS SCHOOL
251 NORTH SAN PEDRO RD.
SAN RAFAEL, CA. 94903

MICHAEL AND THE DENTIST

written and photographed by Bernard Wolf

Four Winds Press   New York

Acknowledgments

The author wishes to thank the following persons for their invaluable assistance during the preparation of this book: Harvey H. Schwaid, D.D.S., New York City, who is affiliated with Lenox Hill Hospital; Maureen Carroll, Dental Assistant; Ana Wolf, the author's wife; and once more, Mike Levins, who prepared the beautiful photographic prints for this book. Most of all, the author is truly indebted to David Reuther of Four Winds Press. Without his wise counsel and patience, this book might not have happened.

We gratefully acknowledge permission to use lines from "Heigh-Ho" (The Dwarfs' Marching Song), music by Frank Churchill and words by Larry Morey, copyright © 1938 by Bourne Co., copyright renewed. All rights reserved. Used by permission.

Library of Congress Cataloging in Publication Data
Wolf, Bernard.
Michael and the dentist.
Summary: Photographs and text record a young boy's
first visit to the dentist to have a cavity filled.
1. Dentistry—Juvenile literature.   2. Children—
Dental care—Juvenile literature   [1. Dentistry]
I. Title.
RK63.W64   617.6   80-12343
ISBN 0-590-07637-X

Published by Four Winds Press
A Division of Scholastic Magazines, Inc., New York, N.Y.
Copyright © 1980 by Bernard Wolf
All rights reserved
Printed in the United States of America
Library of Congress Catalog Card Number: 80-12343

1   2   3   4   5   84   83   82   81   80

For my beloved son, MICHAEL, *with pride and wonderment.*

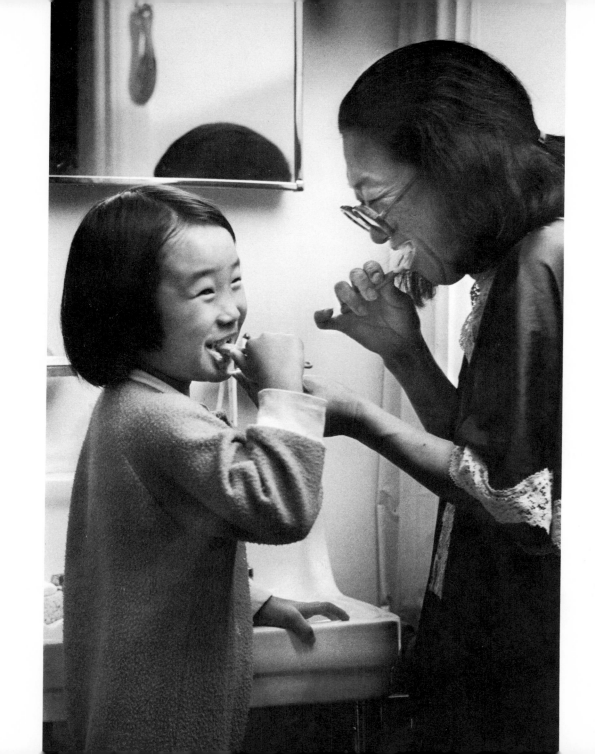

Every night before he goes to bed, Michael and his mother brush their teeth together. This is a race that Michael enjoys winning. He also enjoys his mother's praise when he does an extra good job.

Last month, Michael's mother took him to see a dentist for the very first time. Michael had all of his teeth X-rayed. Then, after a careful examination of his mouth, the dentist showed the X rays to Michael's mother and pointed out four cavities that needed to be cleaned out and filled. Tomorrow, Michael has another appointment with the dentist.

Michael and his mother arrive at the dentist's office at 8:30 in the morning. Michael is a bit grumpy because the dentist has cautioned his mother not to allow Michael to eat or drink anything until after his visit, not even a glass of water. He is also a little nervous because he senses that this visit will be different from the last one.

Since Michael is the first patient of the day, he and his mother have the waiting room all to themselves. He finds an interesting children's book and his mother reads him a story to make the time pass more pleasantly. She has barely finished the story when the receptionist comes in and tells Michael that the dentist is ready to see him now.

Just inside the door of his office
stands Dr. Schwaid with his hand
outstretched and a big smile on his
face. Next to him is his assistant,
Miss Carroll.

"Good morning, Michael," he says.
"How's my new friend today?"

"Fine," replies Michael, "but I sure
am hungry."

"I'll bet you are," says Dr. Schwaid.
"I'll tell you what. If you agree to be
my helper, we can get one of your
teeth fixed up like new in a jiffy. Then
you and your mommy can have a
great big breakfast together. Is it
a deal?"

"Okay," Michael agrees, shaking
Dr. Schwaid's hand.

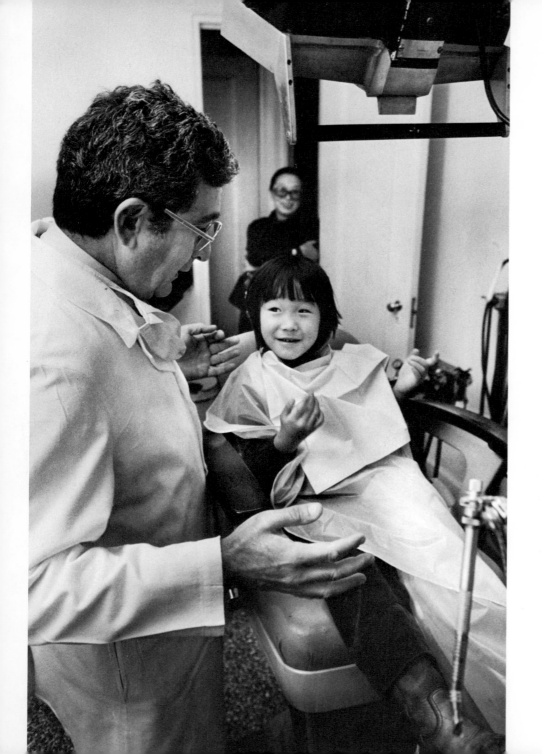

Miss Carroll helps Michael into the dental chair and adjusts it so he is comfortable. Then she fastens a plastic sheet and a napkin around his neck.

"Now tell me, Michael," Dr. Schwaid says, "what kind of chair are you sitting in? Do you remember?"

"I don't know," Michael replies.

"What?" says Dr. Schwaid. "You've forgotten already? I don't believe it!"

"Oh, wait," says Michael. "Now I remember. It's a magic chair!"

"Right!" Dr. Schwaid responds with relief. "I just knew you wouldn't forget an important thing like *that*. But I'll bet you don't remember the magic word to make the chair move."

"Oh, yes, I do," cries Michael. "It's abracadabra!"

"My goodness, Michael," says Dr. Schwaid. "You have an amazing memory." He places his foot gently onto a pedal near the base of the chair. As he depresses the pedal he continues,

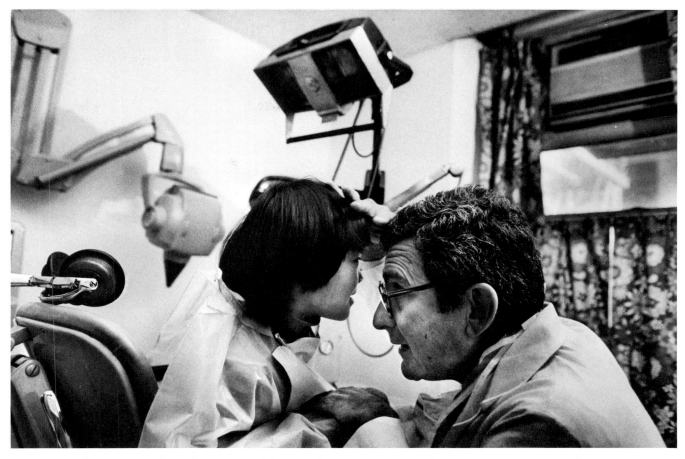

"Repeat these words after me: Abracadabra, magic chair, we command you to rise!"

Michael repeats the words and, sure enough, the chair rises and rises until it can go no further.

Dr. Schwaid quickly stoops down, placing his hand on top of Michael's head. "What on earth have you been eating since the last time I saw you, Michael? Why, you're growing so fast you're even taller than I am!"

"That's silly," giggles Michael. He knows Dr. Schwaid is only playing a game with him. Still, he loves every minute of it. "I'm not taller than you yet, but when I grow up, I will be."

"I'm sure you will, Michael," replies Dr. Schwaid with a smile. He is pleased to see Michael in such a relaxed and happy mood. He wants to make sure that Michael's visit is a pleasant one.

Dr. Schwaid pushes another lever on the floor and this time the chair gradually descends until Michael reaches a comfortable position for Dr. Schwaid to work with him. "Now, what's the magic word that makes Sam come out of hiding?"

Michael looks eagerly at a steel door to the left of his chair. "Abracadabra, come out, Sam!" he commands. To his disappointment, nothing happens.

"I don't think that's the right word, Michael," says Dr. Schwaid.

Michael thinks very hard for a moment. Then he remembers and shouts, "Open sesame! Come out, Sam!"

This time, the steel door slides open silently and out pops an instrument panel full of strange-looking gadgets. Michael claps his hands in delight.

"Good for you, Michael!" says Dr. Schwaid.

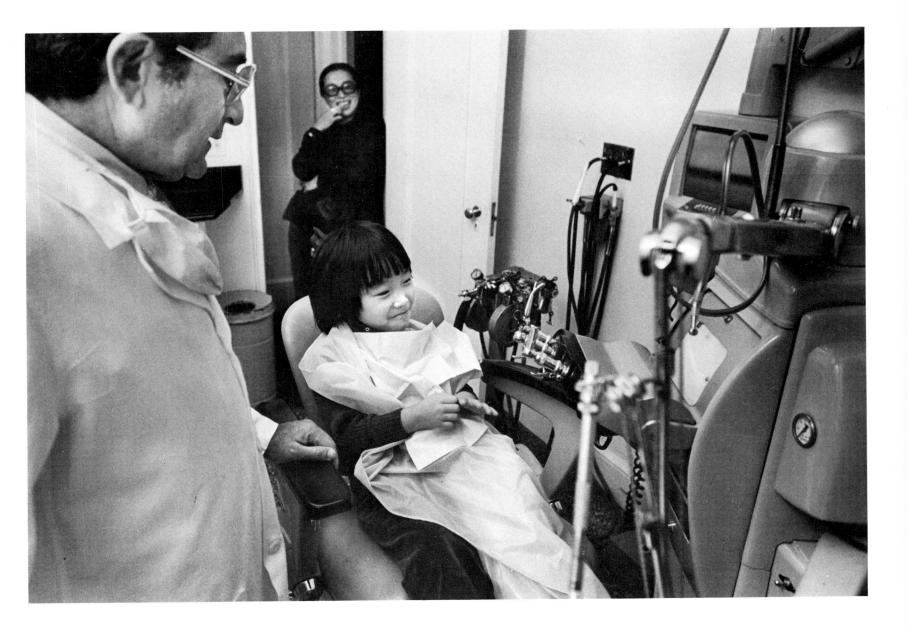

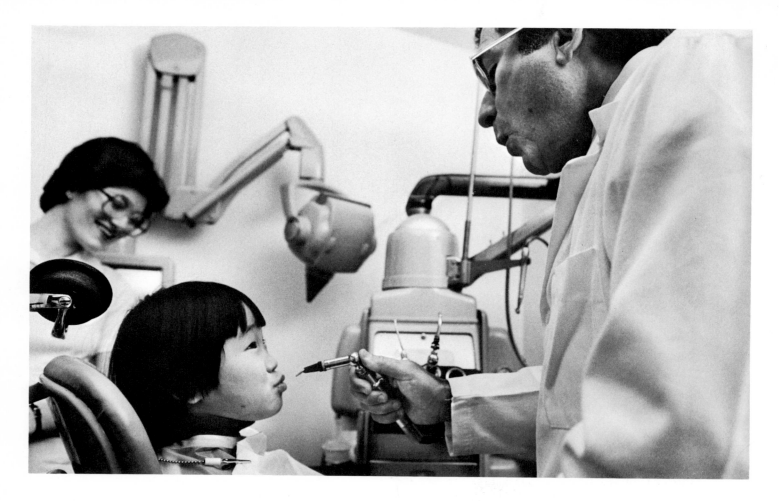

Michael is curious about what everything does, so Dr. Schwaid gives him a demonstration. He begins with the air syringe, first placing it in his own mouth to show Michael that it doesn't hurt. He explains that the syringe is used to blow air onto a tooth to keep it dry. Then he directs the nozzle of the syringe toward Michael's mouth. Michael grins, puckers up his lips, and blows back hard.

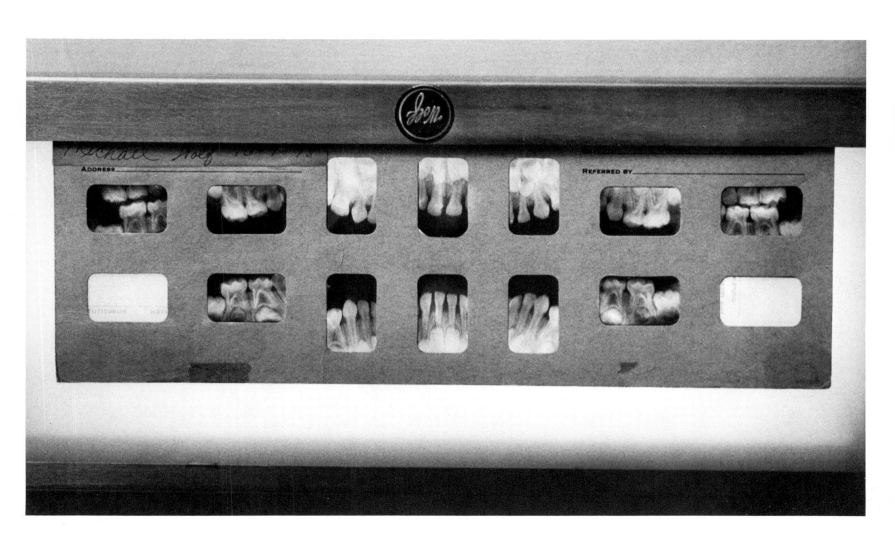

While Dr. Schwaid explains what the other instruments do, Miss Carroll pulls Michael's set of mounted X rays out of the file and places them on the X-ray viewer. When seen like this, the X rays present a fascinating picture. It is as though a tiny photographer had stood on the tip of Michael's tongue and taken photographs of his entire mouth.

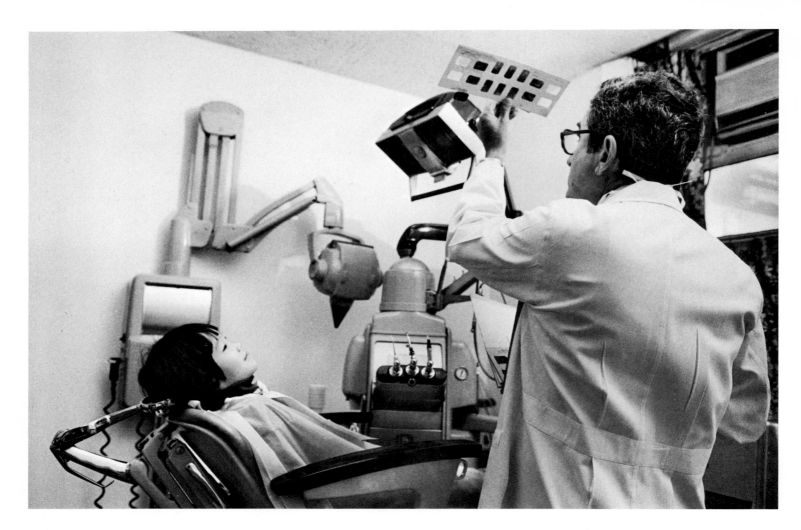

Dr. Schwaid takes a look at the X rays and places them on an illuminated screen behind the open instrument panel at Michael's side. "Tell me, Michael," he says, "do you know what these are?"

Michael grabs a dental probe from the table in front of him while Dr. Schwaid listens attentively. "Sure I do," he replies, using the probe as a

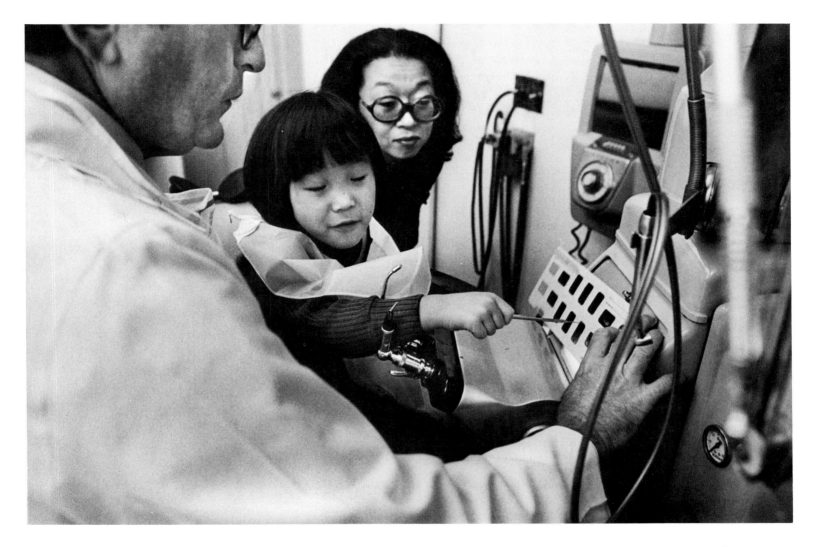

pointer. "See? These are the pictures you took of all my teeth, remember? You told me to sit very still when you took them. And I did, too, didn't I? And now, I bet I know what you're going to do next."

"What's that?" asks Dr. Schwaid.

"You're going to operate on my teeth," says Michael, opening his mouth wide.

"Michael, you're too smart for me. I tell you what. Why don't we change places? You be the dentist and I'll be the patient."

"Aw," responds Michael with a grin, "you're just fooling me."

"Well, okay. This is what we're really going to do," says Dr. Schwaid. "There's a part of your tooth that's sick. So first we have to clean out the stuff that's bothering it, and then we put in a filling to make sure your tooth stays healthy. How does that sound to you?"

"Fine," says Michael.

Dr. Schwaid feels that this is the right moment to prepare Michael for analgesia. An analgesic is different from an anaesthetic. An analgesic allows Dr. Schwaid to work on Michael's tooth without his feeling any pain. It also leaves Michael fully awake and conscious of everything that is going on. Under anaesthesia, a patient is unconscious. Dr. Schwaid wheels out a weird-looking contraption with a lot of hoses attached to it. Michael hasn't really noticed this piece of equipment before. "Michael," says Dr. Schwaid, "I would like you to meet my magic orange machine."

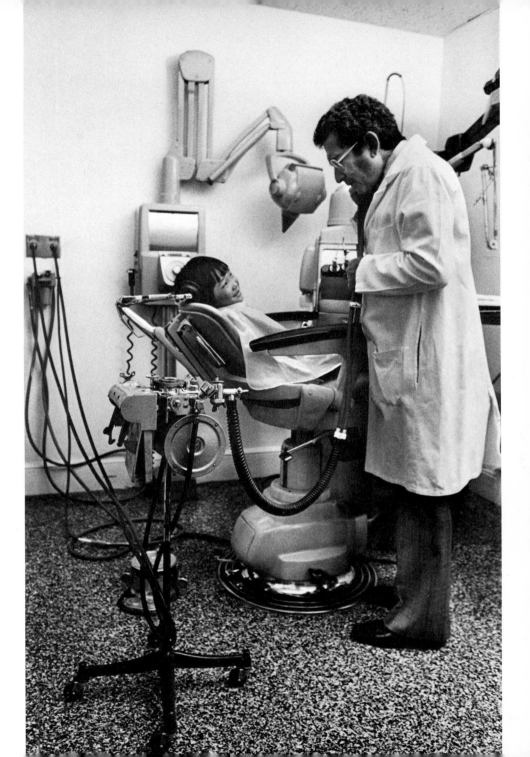

Michael is filled with curiosity about this new wonder. "What does it do?" he asks.

"Why, with this machine, you can visit almost any magic land you like. But first, let's see if Mr. Orange Machine Man is on the line, ready to make your reservation. Okay?"

"Oh, goody!" says Michael.

The machine Dr. Schwaid is working with is a nitrous oxide/oxygen machine. After he fits the nosepiece over Michael's nose and Michael breathes in for a short while, the nitrous oxide/oxygen gas combination will make Michael feel completely relaxed. Dr. Schwaid calls it his orange machine because he rubs some oil of orange into the tubing just behind the nosepiece to give the gas a pleasant fragrance.

Putting the nosepiece to his mouth, Dr. Schwaid speaks into it as he would into a telephone. "Hello, hello? Mr. Orange Machine Man, are you there?" Now he places the nosepiece to his ear and listens. "Oh, there you are. Good. Tell me, what magic lands do you have available for Michael to visit today? What's that? What magic land does he want to go to today? Hold on a minute, please." He places the nosepiece in front of Michael's mouth and says, "I think you'd better tell him yourself, Michael."

Michael thinks carefully for a moment. Then he says, "Umm, let's see. Bicycle Land? No, wait. Magic Car Land! That's what I want!"

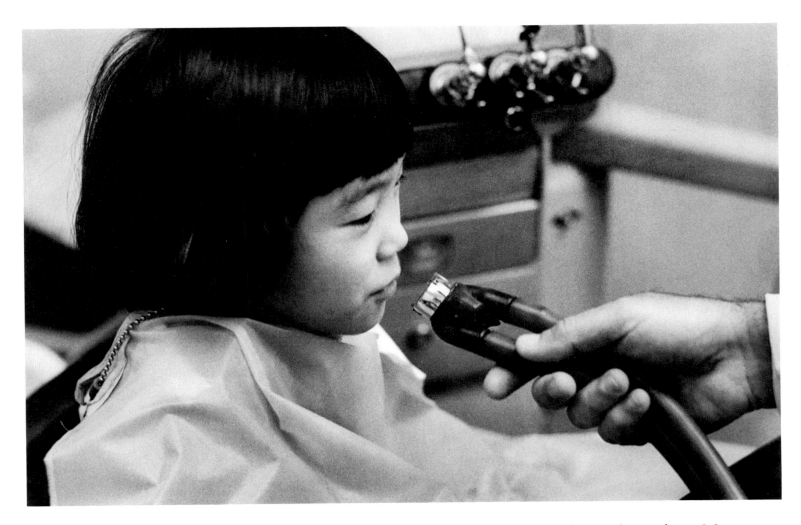

"Magic Car Land? Gee, that sounds like fun. Did you hear that, Mr. Orange Machine Man? Right. Magic Car Land it is," says Dr. Schwaid. "But first, before we can get there, we have to wear an oxygen mask just like the astronauts, see?" Dr. Schwaid fits the nosepiece over his own nose to demonstrate.

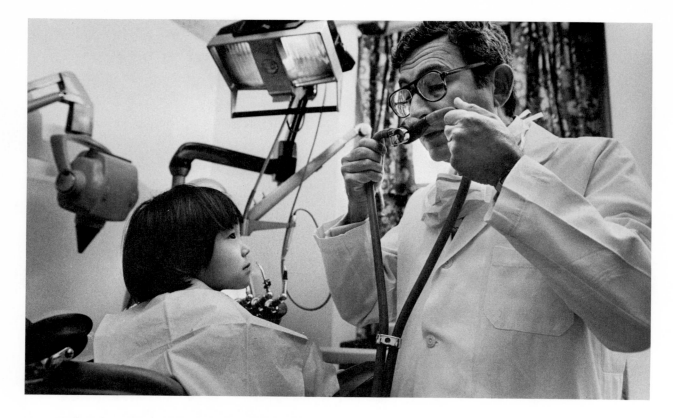

Michael watches intently. For him, the fun of playing this game has suddenly vanished. He doesn't want anything to interfere with his breathing. "I don't want that thing on my nose," he declares.

"Michael, I'm surprised at you," says Dr. Schwaid. "Here we had it all arranged for you to visit Magic Car Land and have a good time."

"I don't care. I don't want to go to Magic Car Land anyway and I don't want that thing on me!"

"Okay, Michael," says Dr. Schwaid. "But then I'll have to use some of my magic water instead." Reaching over to the dental table, Dr. Schwaid picks up

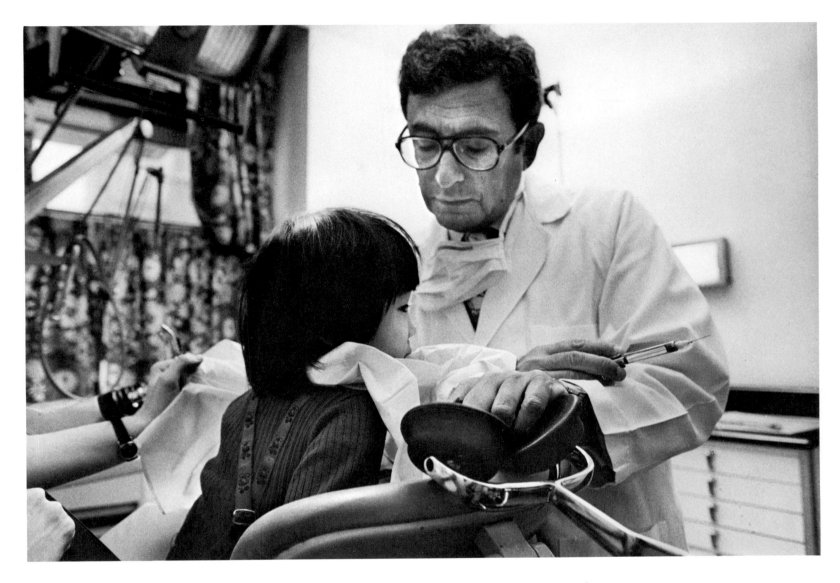

a hypodermic syringe of novocaine and lays it across his arm.

Michael can't take his eyes off the syringe. He's never seen such a big needle in his life. "What are you going to do with *that*?" he whispers.

"I told you," replies Dr. Schwaid. "That's my magic water. It will put your tooth to sleep so we can fix it up like new."

"Uh-uh. You're not sticking that into me. No way!" cries Michael.

"Now look, Michael," Dr. Schwaid says calmly, "if I don't put your tooth to sleep, I can't fix it. So, it's either this or the orange machine. It's up to you, but you have to decide. I still think you would have a lot more fun with Mr. Orange Machine."

"Okay," Michael says quietly, "I'll try the orange machine."

"Hooray for Michael!" cry Dr. Schwaid and Miss Carroll in almost the same breath.

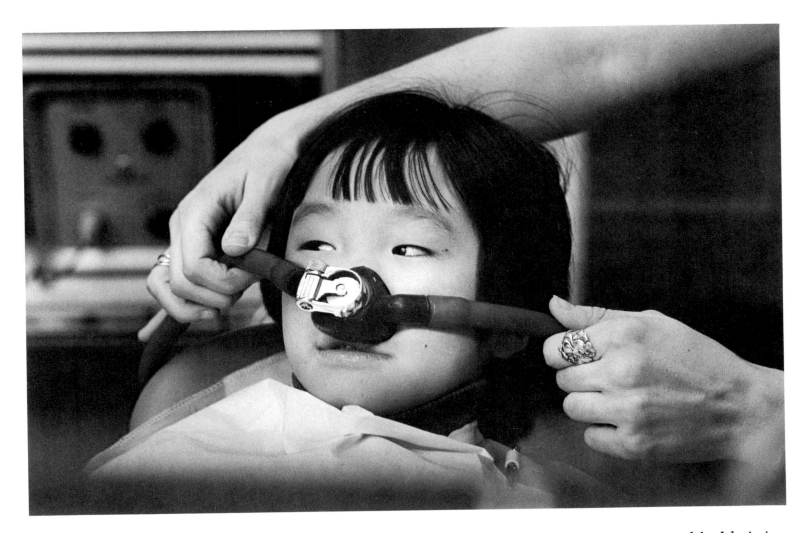

Miss Carroll gently fits the nosepiece over Michael's nose and holds it in place while Dr. Schwaid adjusts the valves on the machine. Michael looks anxiously at his mother for reassurance. After a few moments, his breathing becomes relaxed and regular.

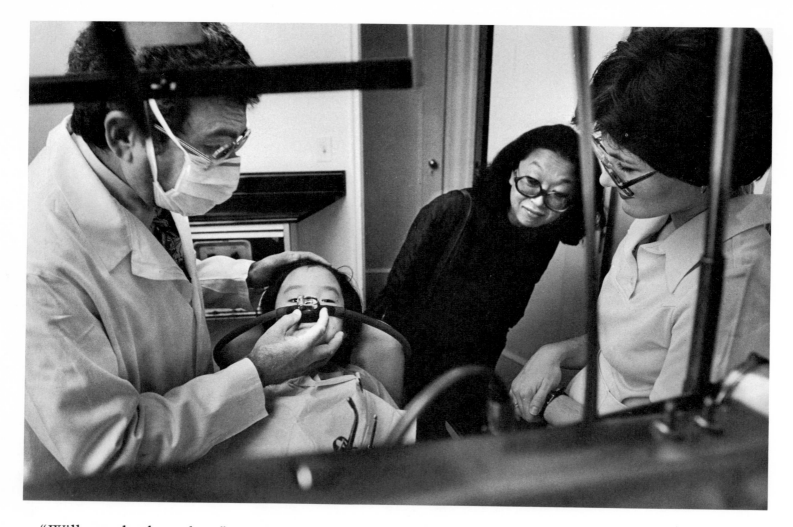

"Will you look at that," says Dr. Schwaid. "Michael, you really do look like an astronaut now." He picks up a large mirror and holds it in front of Michael so that he can see, too. A big, wide grin appears on Michael's face.

"Can you breathe okay, Michael?" asks Dr. Schwaid.

"Uh-huh," Michael nods.

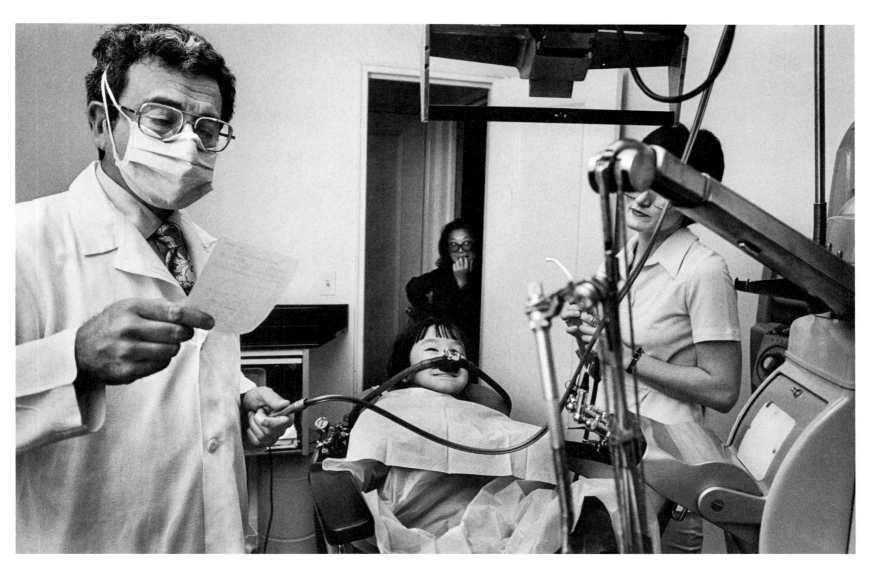

Dr. Schwaid picks up Michael's dental treatment plan for one final look. He wears a mask because the instrument he will use generates a constant spray of water inside the patient's mouth as well as onto the dentist's face.

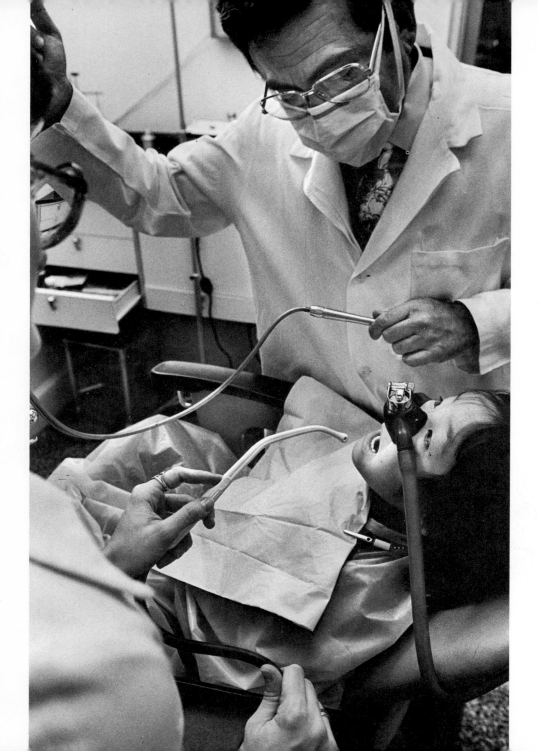

"Open wide, please," says Dr. Schwaid. Miss Carroll holds the nozzle of a suction machine which will remove excess moisture from Michael's mouth.

"What's that in your hand?" Michael asks.

In his left hand, Dr. Schwaid holds the dental drill.

"That's a good question," Dr. Schwaid replies. "This is what I use to clean out your tooth. It works very fast and sprays lots of water to keep your tooth nice and cool while I fix it. Here, feel it yourself." He picks up Michael's index finger and lets him touch the tip of the drill. "See," he adds, "it doesn't hurt. It's just another instrument. Now, are we all set?" Dr. Schwaid directs the dental spotlight so that it shines in Michael's mouth and not in his eyes. "Heigh ho, heigh ho, it's off to work we go...." sings Dr. Schwaid.

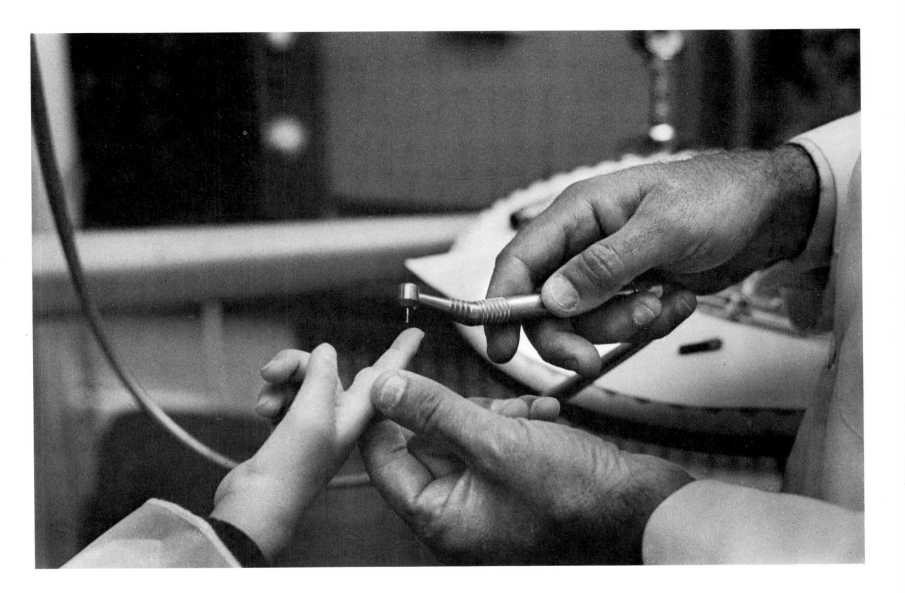

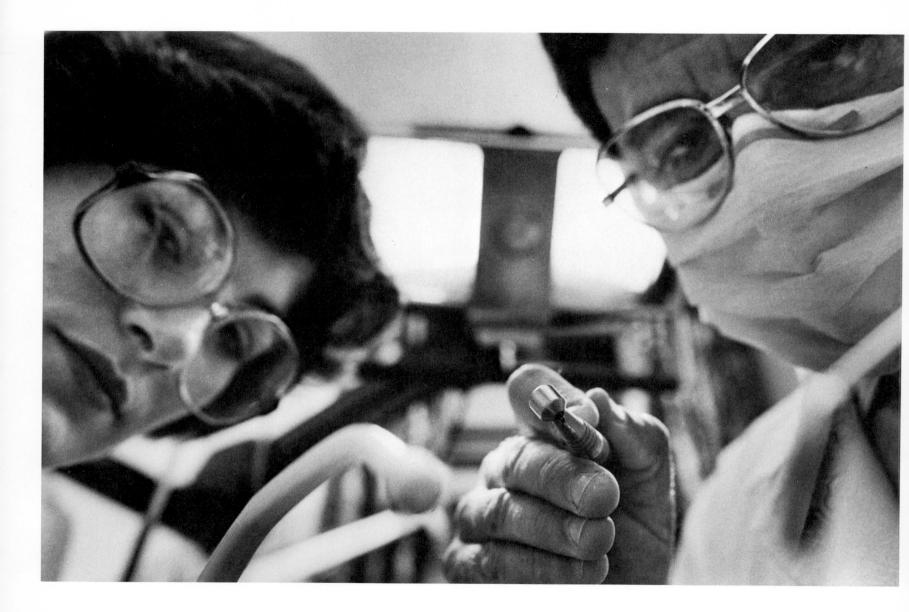

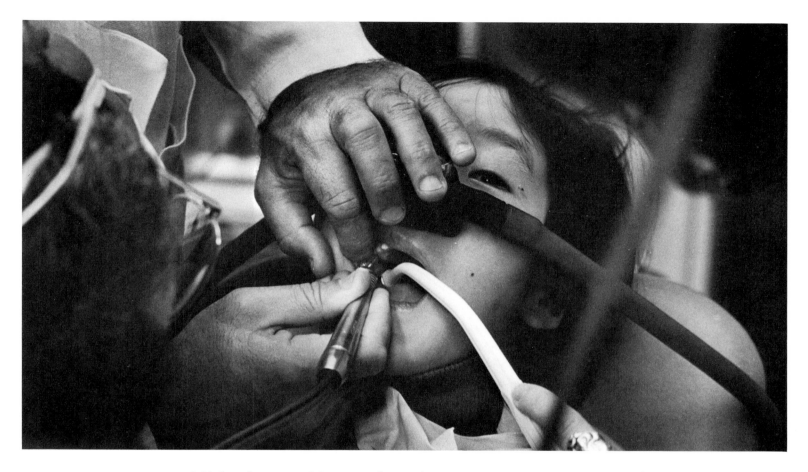

Michael opens his mouth wide. For a moment, his eyes dart nervously
from Miss Carroll to Dr. Schwaid. The next instant, both the suction nozzle
and drill are inside his mouth. Dr. Schwaid continues singing merrily. Michael
is reassured by the sound of his voice. He is aware that something is being
done to his tooth. He can feel the buzzing of the drill, but because of the
nitrous oxide, he is not bothered by pain or discomfort.

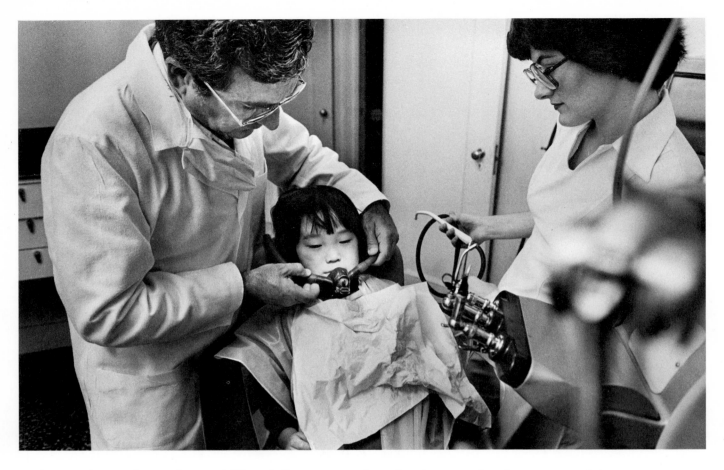

Dr. Schwaid works swiftly. After a couple of minutes, he interrupts his singing and says, "Okay, Mr. Astronaut, it's countdown time. Are you ready? I'll start with the number five; you follow with your fingers. When I get to number one, your tooth will be all cleaned out and we can take off your oxygen mask. Five . . . four . . . three . . . and a two . . . we're almost done . . . and . . . one!" He quickly places the drill out of the way, lowers his face mask, and removes the nosepiece from Michael's nose.

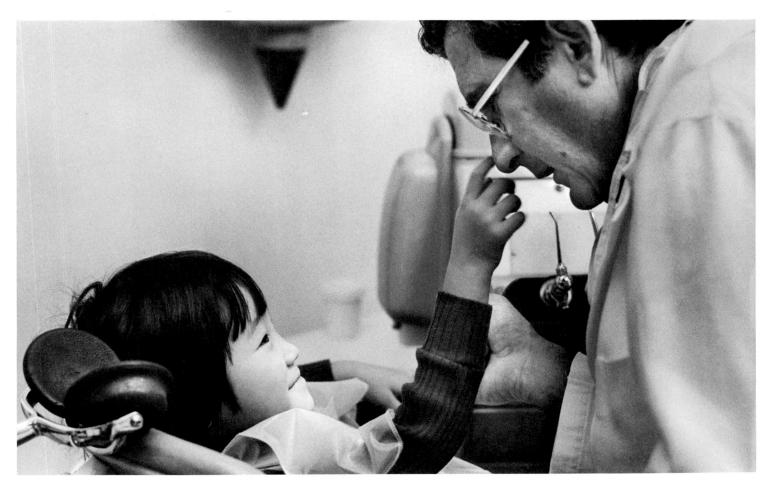

Michael feels a little bit giddy and dazed.

Dr. Schwaid says, "The hard part is all over now, Michael. You did very well. The rest will be easy."

Michael realizes that Dr. Schwaid has kept his promise to remove the nosepiece at the end of the countdown. He reaches up to touch his face gratefully.

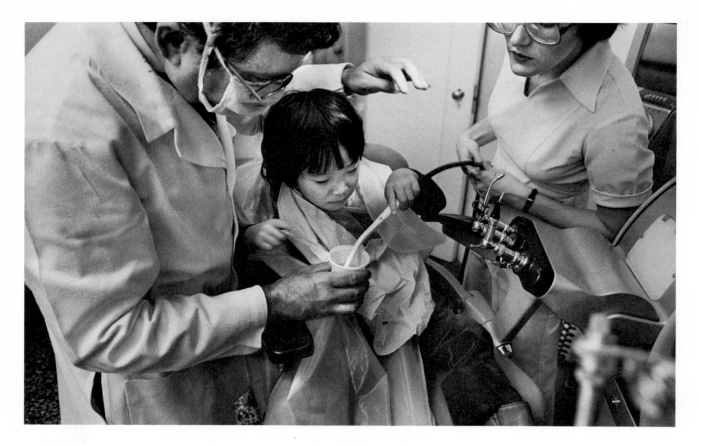

Michael wants to see how the suction nozzle works. Dr. Schwaid fills a cup with water and hands the nozzle to Michael. "It's like a powerful magic straw," he says. "Watch." He turns the machine on and — "whoosh!" — all the water in the cup is sucked up, leaving not even a drop behind!

"Do it again," cries Michael.

"Listen," says Dr. Schwaid, "I'll bet you think I've used up all my magic tricks and don't have any more left."

"Well," says Michael, "do you?"

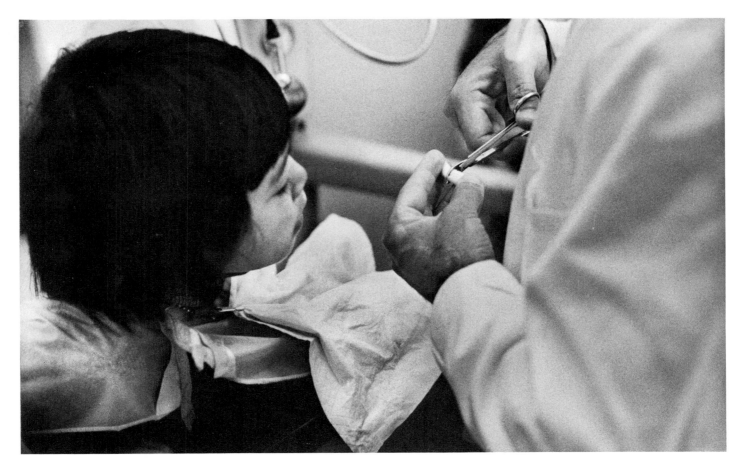

"Ho, ho, ho! Before your very eyes you will see me produce two objects where before there was only one." Dr. Schwaid picks up a cotton roll and snips it in half with a pair of scissors.

"*That's* not a magic trick," says Michael, giggling.

"Maybe not *exactly* magic," replies Dr. Schwaid, "but it worked, didn't it?"

The cotton rolls are placed on either side of Michael's tooth in order to keep the surface clean and dry while the filling is put into place.

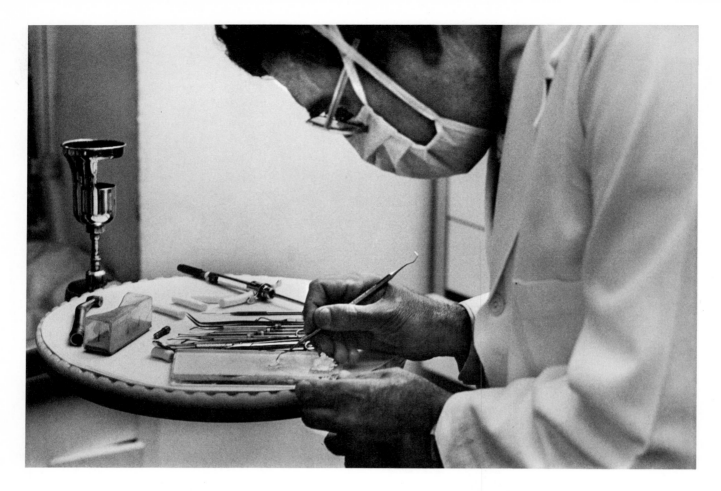

Meanwhile, Miss Carroll mixes a white insulation material on a thick piece of glass. She must do this quickly before the paste has a chance to harden. When it is ready, she places it on Dr. Schwaid's bracket table.

"Are you ready for some of this nice white mud, Michael?" asks Dr. Schwaid.

"What does it do?" Michael wants to know.

"It will stop your tooth from being bothered when you eat or drink very hot or cold things," says Dr. Schwaid.

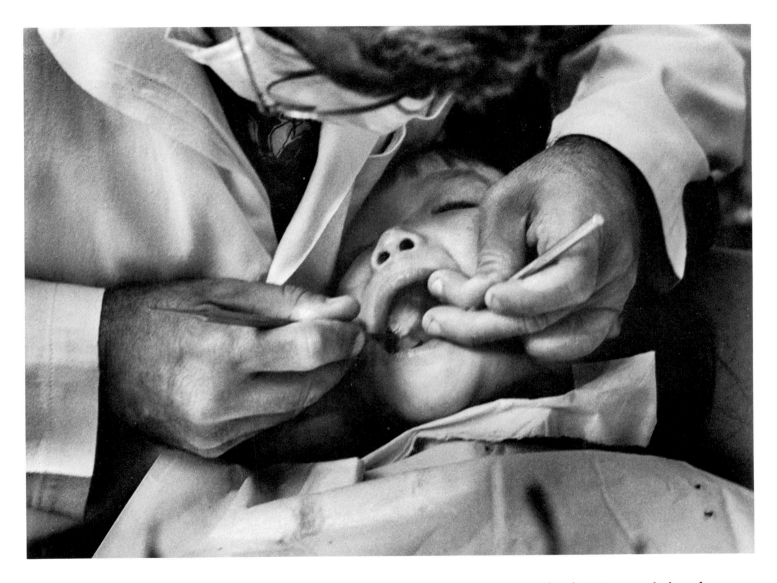

Michael opens his mouth wide without being asked. His tooth has been isolated by the cotton pads, cleaned by air from the air syringe, and swabbed with antiseptic.

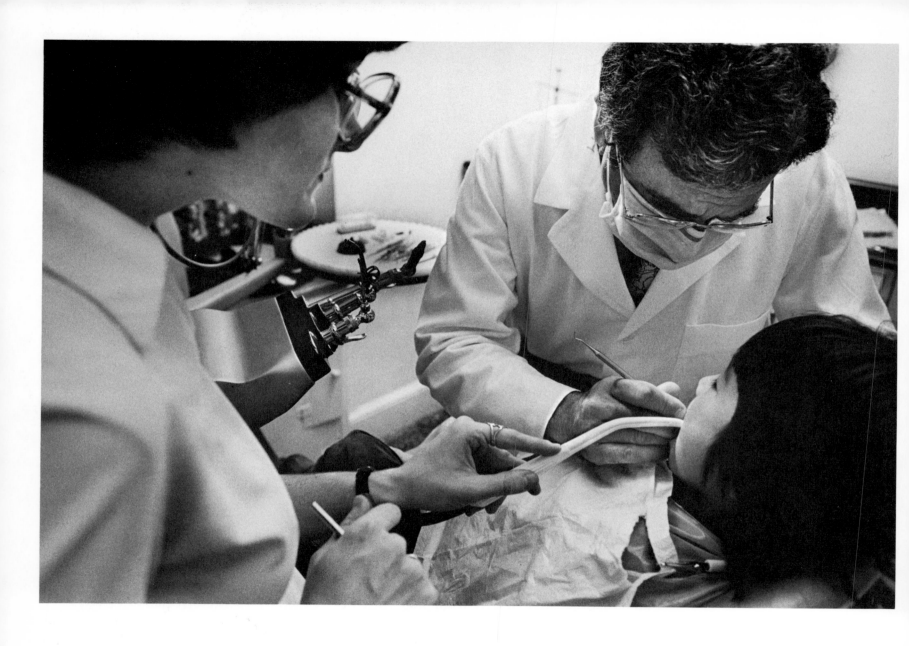

Dr. Schwaid picks up some of the insulating material on the tip of a plugging instrument and puts it into the cavity in his tooth.

Now it's time for the filling. Miss Carroll mixes the silver amalgam filling material in a machine and places it on the bracket table. Dr. Schwaid explains that he is going to fill Michael's tooth with silver. Even though he is growing a little tired at this point, Michael is still curious.

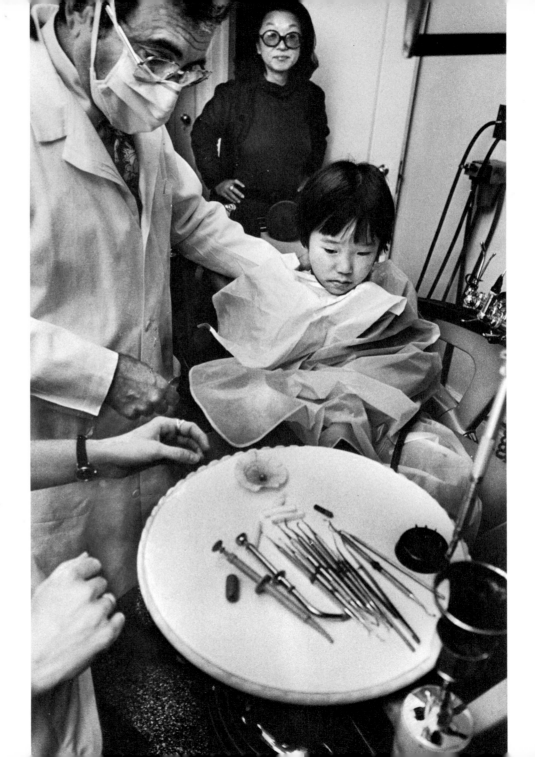

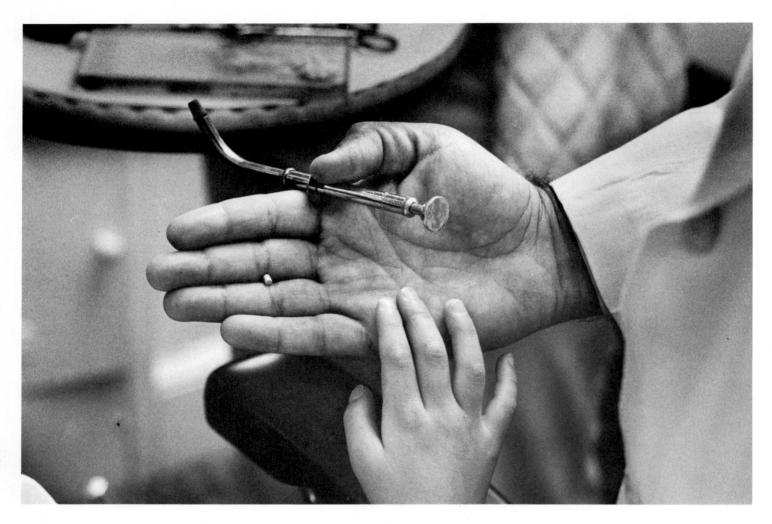

"Let's see," he says. "Is that really *real* silver?"

"Of course it's real," answers Dr. Schwaid. "Do you think I'd use *fake* silver on you? Not on my friend Michael! No, sir!"

Dr. Schwaid begins to fill Michael's tooth. Using a special tool called an amalgam carrier, he squeezes the silver into Michael's cavity.

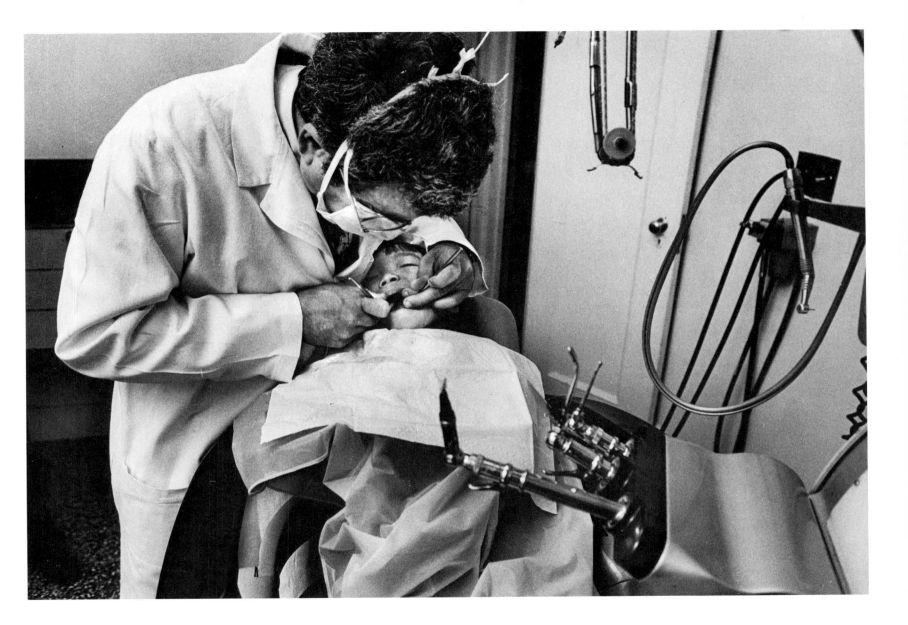

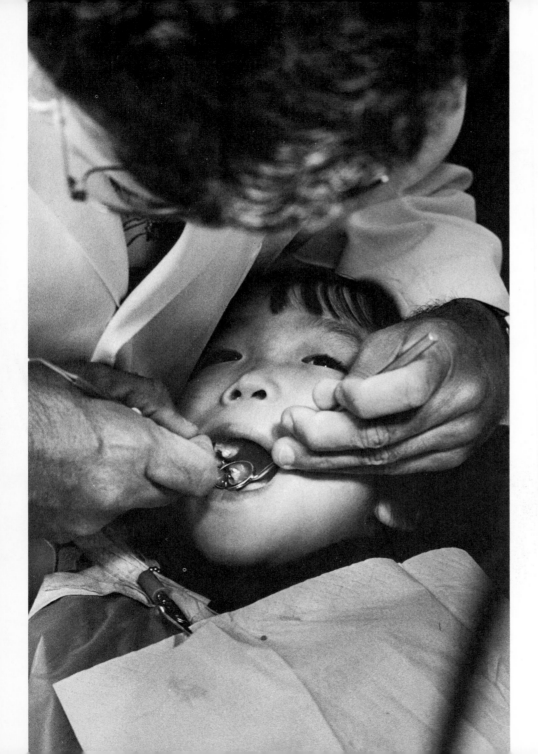

Next, with the aid of a small mirror to see what he is doing, he carves the silver into the natural shape that a normal tooth has. Inside Michael's head, there is a strange squeaking feeling as the silver is scraped into place.

Michael is cooperating beautifully. Dr. Schwaid asks him to try to breathe only through his nose and not his mouth. Breathing through his mouth would fog the mirror.

Soon Dr. Schwaid removes his instruments from Michael's mouth and says, "Guess what?"

With his mouth still open, Michael says, "Wha—?"

"We're all done! And you were just great!"

"Really?" asks Michael with relief.

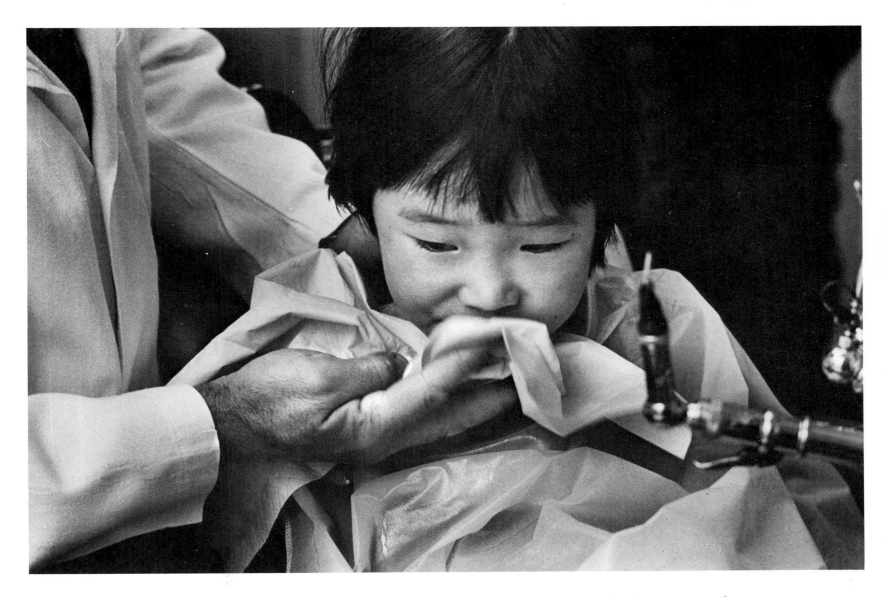

Dr. Schwaid holds the napkin for him while Michael spits out the excess particles of silver. Then he asks Michael to rinse out his mouth.

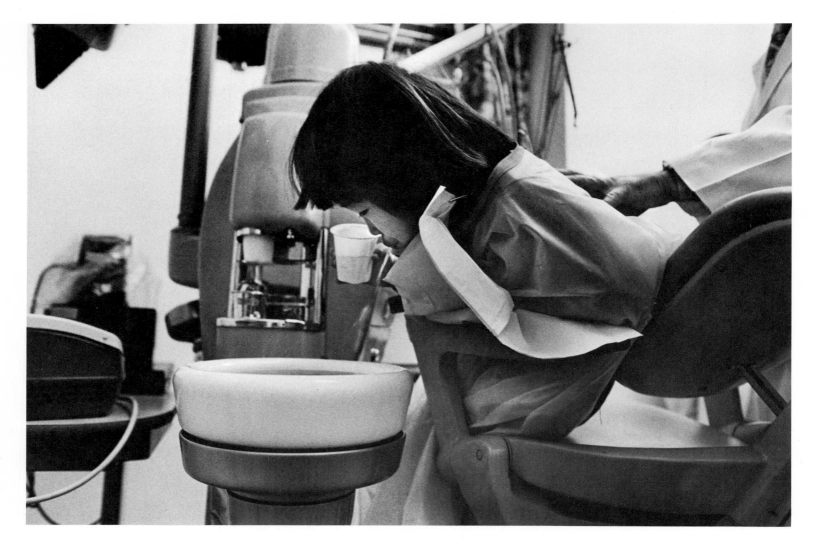

While he is busy at the water fountain, Dr. Schwaid discovers the teddy bear Michael has been clutching in his lap all through this session. As Michael finishes rinsing his mouth, he finds Dr. Schwaid examining the teddy bear's teeth.

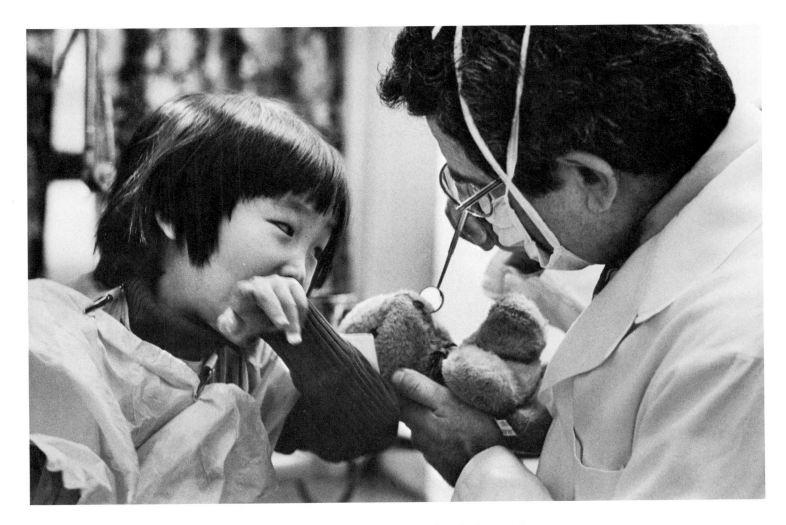

"What are you doing?" asks Michael, laughing.

"Well, now that *you* have a brand new filling, I'm wondering if Mr. Bear might need one, too. What do you think, Michael?"

"Teddy bears don't have cavities," scoffs Michael. "Only real kids do. You know that!"

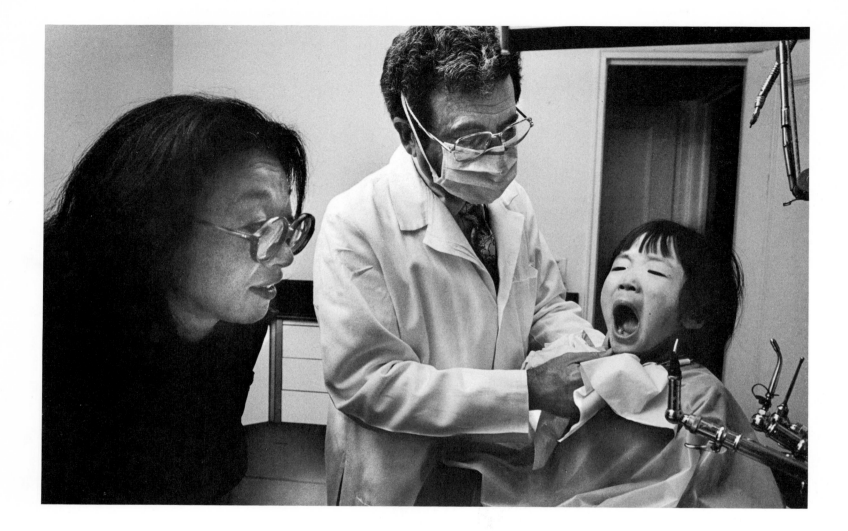

"Maybe you're right." Dr. Schwaid laughs. "I'll think about it. But meanwhile, how about showing Mommy your shiny new filling?"

Michael proudly opens his mouth as wide as it will go as his mother peers inside.

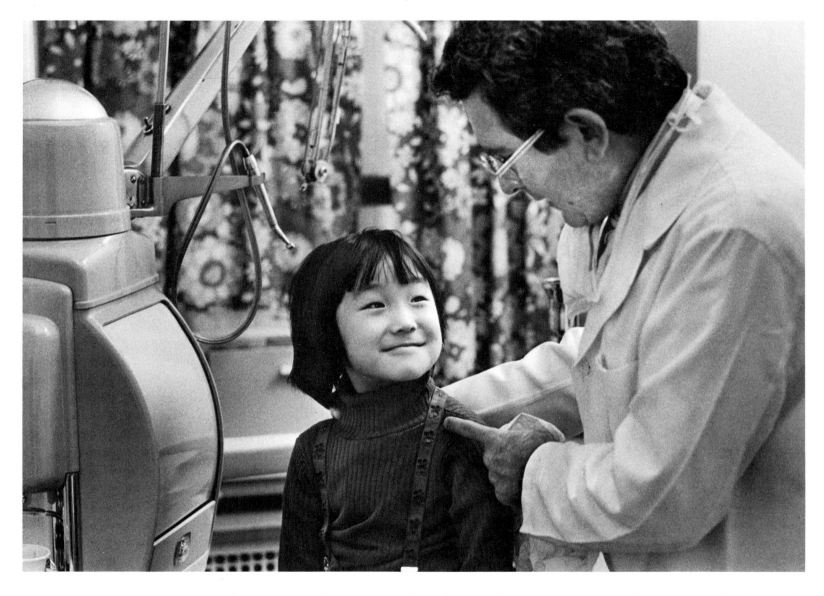

Dr. Schwaid removes the plastic sheet and napkin from around Michael's neck and says, "Michael, you've been one of the best helpers I've ever had.

"Now, until the next time I see you, I'm still going to need your help. Can you guess what I would like you to remember to do?"

"I know," says Michael with a smile. "You want me to brush my teeth after every meal and not eat too much candy and sweet stuff."

"That settles it!" Dr. Schwaid declares. "You're such a good patient, I think you deserve a prize! Miss Carroll, would you bring in the treasure chest, please?"

To Michael's delight, Miss Carroll places a large cardboard treasure chest on the floor and opens it. Inside are all sorts of small toys. Michael rummages through the box for a moment and selects a toy car. Looking up at Dr. Schwaid, he asks, "Can I keep this?"

"You certainly can, Michael." Dr. Schwaid smiles. "Enjoy it and enjoy your meal, too. See you next week and thanks again for your help."

Once outside Dr. Schwaid's office, Michael's mother makes a beeline to the nearest restaurant where she buys a hamburger with french fries for each of them. When they are seated at a table, she turns to Michael and says, "You know, you've made me very, very proud of you today, Michael."

"How come, Mommy?" Michael asks.

"Because you did a very important thing at Dr. Schwaid's office. Even though you were a little nervous, you were brave enough to help him finish his work. That's why I'm proud of you."

"You know what?" says Michael, his eyes sparkling. "I think you're the best mommy in the whole, wide world!"

By the same author

In This Proud Land
Adam Smith Goes to School
Anna's Silent World
Connie's New Eyes
Don't Feel Sorry for Paul
Tinker and the Medicine Men
Daniel and the Whale Hunters
Jamaica Boy
The Little Weaver of Agato